DATE DUE		

SCIENCEWORKS!

Be a Volcanologist

By Suzy Gazlay

Volcanology Consultant: Robert B. Trombley, Ph.D.

Series Consultant: Kirk A. Janowiak

Gareth Stevens
Publishing

Please visit our web site at www.garethstevens.com. For a free catalog describing our list of high-quality books, call 1-800-542-2595 (USA) or 1-800-387-3178 (Canada). Our fax: 1-877-542-2596

Library of Congress Cataloging-in-Publication Data available upon request from publisher.
ISBN-13: 978-0-8368-8930-7 (lib. bdg.)
ISBN-10: 0-8368-8930-4 (lib. bdg.)
ISBN-13: 978-0-8368-8937-6 (softcover)
ISBN-10: 0-8368-8937-1 (softcover)

This North American edition first published in 2008 by
Gareth Stevens Publishing
A Weekly Reader® Company
1 Reader's Digest Road
Pleasantville, NY 10570-7000 USA

This U.S. edition copyright © 2008 by Gareth Stevens, Inc. Original edition copyright © 2007 by ticktock Media Ltd.
First published in Great Britain in 2007 by ticktock Media Ltd., Unit 2, Orchard Business Centre, North Farm Road,
Tunbridge Wells, Kent, TN2 3XF United Kingdom

ticktock Project Editor: Jo Hanks and Joe Harris
ticktock Designer: James Powell
With thanks to: Sara Greasley and Anna Brett

Gareth Stevens Editor: Jayne Keedle
Gareth Stevens Creative Director: Lisa Donovan
Gareth Stevens Graphic Designer: Keith Plechaty

Printed in the United States of America

1 2 3 4 5 6 7 8 9 10 09 08 07

SUZY GAZLAY

Suzy Gazlay (M.A. Integrated Math/Science Education) is a teacher and writer who has worked with students of all ages. She has also served as a science specialist, curriculum developer, and consultant in varying capacities. She is the recipient of a Presidential Award for Excellence in Math and Science Teaching. Now retired from full-time classroom teaching, she continues to write, consult, and work with educators and children, particularly in science and music education. Her many interests include music, environmental issues, marine biology, and the outdoors.

KIRK A. JANOWIAK

Kirk A. Janowiak (B.S. Biology & Natural Resources, M.S. Ecology & Animal Behavior, M.S. Science Education) has enjoyed teaching students from pre-school through college. He has been awarded the National Association of Biology Teachers' Outstanding Biology Teacher Award and was honored to be a finalist for the Presidential Award for Excellence in Math and Science Teaching. Kirk currently teaches Biology and Environmental Science and enjoys a wide range of interests from music to the art of roasting coffee.

ROBERT B. TROMBLEY, PH.D.

Robert B. Trombley is the Principal Research Volcanologist of the International Volcano Research Center and a registered volcanologist. He is an award-winning scientist and has spent 42 years in the field. "R.B," has written several papers and authored two books and has also written several articles for various volcano-related publications. Dr. Trombley has also served as one of the Technical Advisors to the National Geographic Society on a TV documentary about volcanoes. Dr. Trombley is a Professor Emeritus at the Phoenix, Arizona, campus of DeVry University.

CONTENTS

This book will help students develop these vital science skills:

- Gaining abilities necessary to do scientific inquiry
- Understanding scientific inquiry
- Understanding properties of objects and materials
- Identifying position and motion of objects
- Understanding light, heat, and electricity
- Identifying properties of earth materials
- Identifying objects in the sky
- Recognizing changes in earth and sky
- Understanding abilities of technological design
- Understanding about science and technology
- Distinguishing between natural objects and objects made by humans
- Understanding personal health
- Identifying characteristics and changes in populations
- Identifying types of resources
- Identifying changes in environments
- Using science and technology in local challenges
- Understanding science as a human endeavor

Supports the National Science Education Standards (NSES) for Grades K–4

HOW TO USE THIS BOOK

Science is important in the lives of people everywhere. We use science at home and at school. In fact, we use it all the time. You need to know science to understand how the world works. A volcanologist needs to understand science. Volcanologists use science to try to tell when a volcano will erupt. This helps protect people from the dangers of an eruption. With this book, you will get the chance to use science to follow a volcanic eruption.

This exciting science book is very easy to use. Check out what's inside!

INTRODUCTION

Do you have what it takes to be a volcanologist? Find out as you track and study volcanic eruptions!

FACTFILE

Read easy-to-understand information about how volcanoes work.

LAVA FLOWS

Your plane lands on the Big Island of Hawaii. You are here to see one of the most active volcanoes in the world! Kilauea (kee-lah-WAY-uh), a shield volcano, has been erupting for more than 20 years. Recently its lava flow has been increasing. Some local scientists have been studying earthquakes in the area. They meet you at the airport. You jump into their van and head out to a spot where lava is oozing across a road.

FACTFILE

- Lava can be as hot as 2,200° Fahrenheit (1,200° Celsius).
- Kilauea has been erupting since 1983. The lava from its cone flows almost 7 miles (11 km) and falls into the Pacific Ocean.
- *Kilauea* is a Hawaiian word that means "spreading" or "spewing."

10

WORKSTATION

Learn how to interpret volcano data from diagrams, charts, graphs, and maps.

CHALLENGE QUESTIONS

Now that you understand the science, put it into practice.

WORKSTATION

Types of Lava

From the van, you see a fiery river of molten lava making its way down the slope. Up near the summit, fire fountains of lava shoot into the air. The lava rains down like a glowing curtain. Lava can be described by the way that it flows and cools.

- **Pahoehoe (pah-HOH-ee-hoh-ee) lava** is thin and flows smoothly. It moves forward in globs that break out from under a cooled crust. Some pahoehoe lava looks like twisted ropes when it cools.

- **Aa (ah-AH) lava** is thick and sticky. It flows more slowly. Its surface is rough with chunks of broken lava. When it cools, it is jagged and sharp enough to cut through your shoes!

- **Pillow lava** is the most common type of lava. It forms when molten lava comes into contact with water. As the lava cools, it forms mounds that are shaped like pillows. Pillow lava covers much of the ocean floor.

This lava is hot enough to melt the road and cause trees to burst into flames!

Q CHALLENGE QUESTIONS

1. How hot can lava get?
2. Look at the chart above. Which type of lava is most common?
3. Which type of lava has sharp edges when it cools?
4. Which type of lava would you find underwater?
5. Which type of lava flows most smoothly?

11

IF YOU NEED HELP!

TIPS FOR SCIENCE SUCCESS

On page 30, you will find lots of tips to help you with your science work.

ANSWERS

Turn to page 31 to check your answers. (*Try all the activities and questions before you take a look at the answers.*)

GLOSSARY

Turn to page 32 for definitions of volcanology words and science words.

VOLCANOLOGIST ON DUTY

You've been awake now for nearly 24 hours. Your attention is focused on a volcano that is erupting in front of you. You keep an eye on the computers and instruments around you. They tell you what is going on at the volcano. They make it possible for you to watch the eruption from the safety of this observatory. As a volcanologist, you study volcanoes like this one to understand more about how they work. What you learn may help save lives.

FACTFILE

Volcanoes are put into three classes.

- An **active volcano** is one that has erupted at least once during the last 10,000 years.

- A **dormant volcano**, or sleeping volcano, is active, but it hasn't erupted for several hundred years. It may show signs of activity, such as escaping gas.

- An **extinct volcano** is one that hasn't erupted for at least 10,000 years. It is highly unlikely to erupt again.

This dormant volcano is located at Haleakala (ha-lay-ah-kah-LAH) National Park in Hawaii.

Inside a Volcano

A volcano is a vent, or an opening, in Earth's crust. The crust is the thin, hard outer layer of our planet. A volcano may be on land or underwater.

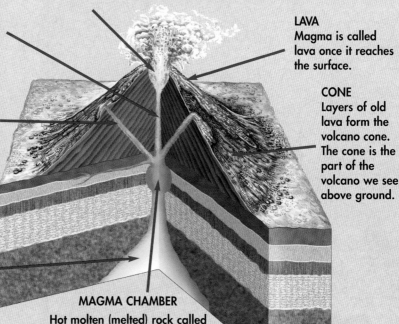

CHIMNEY
Magma mixes with gases from melted rock. It rises up the chimney.

CRATER
Gases, ash, and pieces of hardened lava are shot from the crater. They form a cloud that rises above the volcano.

LAVA
Magma is called lava once it reaches the surface.

SIDE VENT
Magma may branch off to erupt through a side vent. A side vent is an opening in the side of the mountain.

CONE
Layers of old lava form the volcano cone. The cone is the part of the volcano we see above ground.

GASES
Pressure from gases builds until it triggers an explosion.

MAGMA CHAMBER
Hot molten (melted) rock called magma rises into a magma chamber below the volcano. Pressure builds as the magma pushes against the rock.

Q CHALLENGE QUESTIONS

During the eruption, you pick up your camera and watch through the lens as you take pictures.

1. You see the first signs of molten rock flowing down the mountain. What is this molten rock called? What was it called before it reached the surface?

2. Through which passage did the molten rock go between the magma chamber and the crater?

3. What is in the cloud that is growing higher and higher above the volcano?

4. You live near an extinct volcano. Should you be worried about it erupting? Why or why not?

VARIETIES OF VOLCANOES

You've collected all the data you need from the eruption. Now you're off to check on another volcano. This trip will take you halfway around the world! You settle back in the plane and look out the window. The rugged land below you is a volcanic field. A lot of volcanic activity has taken place here. You spot a volcano and then another. You know this area well. You've explored several sections at ground level. Now you're getting a very different view as you look at it from the air.

FACTFILE

There are three main types of volcanoes.

- **Shield:** A shield volcano is large and has sloping sides. It erupts more slowly than other types of volcanoes. The lava is fluid and flows quietly. The sides are built up as the lava hardens.

- **Cinder cone:** This volcano is cone-shaped and has steep sides. Hardened bits of lava land near the vent and build up the sides. Usually it has a bowl-shaped crater.

- **Strato:** A stratovolcano is cone-shaped with steep sides. It gives off gases, ash, and rocks. Its sides are built of layers of lava, ash, and volcanic rocks. These are the most common volcanoes on Earth's surface.

Types of Eruptions

An active volcano may behave in a number of different ways. It may simply give off steam and other gases. It may or may not have a lava flow. It might be explosive. These are the most common types of eruptions, going from the calmest to the most violent.

- **Hawaiian:** This type of eruption produces a quiet flowing of thin, fluid lava. It may erupt as a fountain.

- **Strombolian:** This noisy eruption makes short blasts at regular times. It spits out lava and all sizes of tephra. Tephra is solid rock material thrown into the air during an eruption. Tephra may be fine volcanic ash or large chunks of cooled lava. The volcano may produce thick, sticky lava.

- **Vulcanian:** This eruption often begins by blowing away part of the mountain. A series of loud explosions may follow for a few hours. Ash and tephra are blasted skyward at high speed. A thick ash cloud rises from the peak.

- **Vesuvian:** This eruption can last for days. Huge amounts of ash and gases are blasted out at several hundred miles per hour. An umbrella-shaped ash cloud rises high into the atmosphere. Ash and a lightweight volcanic rock called pumice fall to the ground over a wide area.

- **Pelean:** This type of eruption is very destructive. A blast of steam, gas, lava, and red-hot ash shoots from the volcano. Fiery lava falls back to the ground and travels downhill as fast as 100 miles (160 kilometers) per hour.

Q CHALLENGE QUESTIONS

1. How are the sides of a cinder cone built up?

2. How are the sides of a stratovolcano built up?

3. Look at the chart above. Which type of eruption is more violent: Strombolian or Pelean?

4. What type of eruption shown in the chart above is likely to come from a shield volcano?

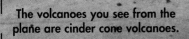
The volcanoes you see from the plane are cinder cone volcanoes.

LAVA FLOWS

Your plane lands on the Big Island of Hawaii. You are here to see one of the most active volcanoes in the world! Kilauea (kee-lah-WAY-uh), a shield volcano, has been erupting for more than 20 years. Recently its lava flow has been increasing. Some local scientists have been studying earthquakes in the area. They meet you at the airport. You jump into their van and head out to a spot where lava is oozing across a road.

FACTFILE

- Lava can be as hot as 2,200° Fahrenheit (1,200° Celsius).

- Kilauea has been erupting since 1983. The lava from its cone flows almost 7 miles (11 km) and falls into the Pacific Ocean.

- *Kilauea* is a Hawaiian word that means "spreading" or "spewing."

WORKSTATION

Types of Lava

From the van, you see a fiery river of molten lava making its way down the slope. Up near the summit, fire fountains of lava shoot into the air. The lava rains down like a glowing curtain. Lava can be described by the way that it flows and cools.

- **Pahoehoe (pah-HOH-ee-hoh-ee) lava** is thin and flows smoothly. It moves forward in globs that break out from under a cooled crust. Some pahoehoe lava looks like twisted ropes when it cools.

- **Aa (ah-AH) lava** is thick and sticky. It flows more slowly. Its surface is rough with chunks of broken lava. When it cools, it is jagged and sharp enough to cut through your shoes!

- **Pillow lava** is the most common type of lava. It forms when molten lava comes into contact with water. As the lava cools, it forms mounds that are shaped like pillows. Pillow lava covers much of the ocean floor.

This lava is hot enough to melt the road and cause trees to burst into flames!

Q CHALLENGE QUESTIONS

1. How hot can lava get?
2. Look at the chart above. Which type of lava is most common?
3. Which type of lava has sharp edges when it cools?
4. Which type of lava would you find underwater?
5. Which type of lava flows most smoothly?

VOLCANIC ISLAND

After studying Kilauea's lava flows for several days, you hear about another volcano that could be ready to erupt. You hop on a plane and head for a remote island in the Pacific. You're excited to see how big this eruption will be! You plan to track how long the eruption lasts. You'll measure the height of the ash cloud over the vent and the volume of ash it produces. Those factors are part of the Volcanic Explosivity Index (VEI). That's the scale scientists use to measure the size of an eruption.

FACTFILE

- The Volcanic Explosivity Index (VEI) is a scale that runs from 0 (low) to 8 (high). Most eruptions have a VEI between 0 and 5.
- This table shows some of the factors used to measure an eruption.

VEI	Description of Volcanic Eruption	Height of the Ash Cloud	How Often It Erupts
0	Non-explosive	Less than 100 meters	Daily
1	Gentle	100–1,000 m	Daily
2	Explosive	1–5 kilometers	Weekly
3	Severe	3–15 km	Yearly
4	Cataclysmic (extremely violent)	10–25 km	10 years or more
5	Paroxysmal (suddenly violently explosive)	over 25 km	50 years or more
6	Colossal (huge)	over 25 km	100 years+
7	Super-colossal	over 25 km	1,000 years+
8	Mega-colossal	over 25 km	10,000 years+

You wonder how this volcano's eruption will measure up against other volcanoes on the Volcanic Explosivity Index.

Volcano	Unzen	Cerro Hudson	Mount Pinatubo
Location	Japan	Chile	Philippines
VEI	4	5	6
Eruption Year	1990	1991	1991

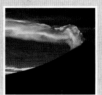

Volcano	Hekla	Ulawun	Reventador
Location	Iceland	Papua New Guinea	Ecuador
VEI	3	4	4
Eruption Year	2000	2000	2002

Volcano	Galeras	Reventador	Cleveland
Location	Colombia	Ecuador	Alaska
VEI	3	2	3
Eruption Year	2004	2004	2006

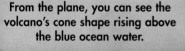

From the plane, you can see the volcano's cone shape rising above the blue ocean water.

CHALLENGE QUESTIONS

1. Look at the chart on page 12. How tall is the ash cloud created by a volcano with a VEI of 3? How often does a volcano with a VEI of 6 erupt?
2. Look at the chart above. Which volcano in the chart had the strongest eruption? What was its VEI?
3. Which volcano erupted twice within two years?

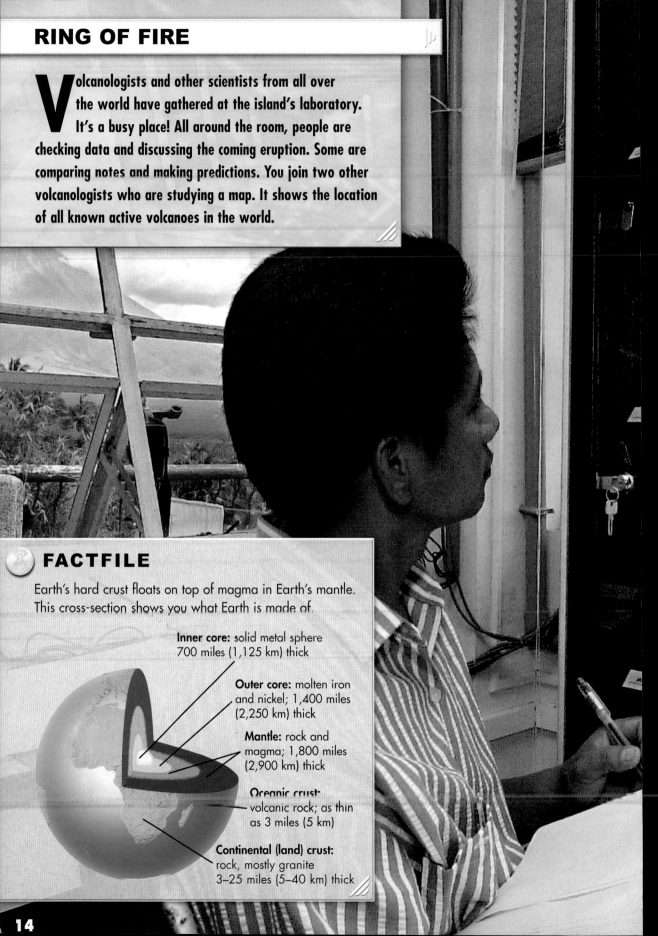

RING OF FIRE

Volcanologists and other scientists from all over the world have gathered at the island's laboratory. It's a busy place! All around the room, people are checking data and discussing the coming eruption. Some are comparing notes and making predictions. You join two other volcanologists who are studying a map. It shows the location of all known active volcanoes in the world.

FACTFILE

Earth's hard crust floats on top of magma in Earth's mantle. This cross-section shows you what Earth is made of.

Inner core: solid metal sphere 700 miles (1,125 km) thick

Outer core: molten iron and nickel; 1,400 miles (2,250 km) thick

Mantle: rock and magma; 1,800 miles (2,900 km) thick

Oceanic crust: volcanic rock; as thin as 3 miles (5 km)

Continental (land) crust: rock, mostly granite 3–25 miles (5–40 km) thick

WORKSTATION

Tectonic Plates

- Most volcanoes form along faults. A fault is crack in Earth's crust. Faults are found where tectonic plates meet. Tectonic plates are giant pieces of Earth's crust. They move on top of a flowing layer in the mantle.
- Earth's tectonic plates fit together like a jigsaw puzzle.
- The plates are in constant slow motion, pushing together and pulling apart. As the plates move, magma seeps through the crust, forming a volcano.
- About 75 percent of the world's active and dormant volcanoes are located around the Pacific Ocean. This region is called the Ring of Fire.

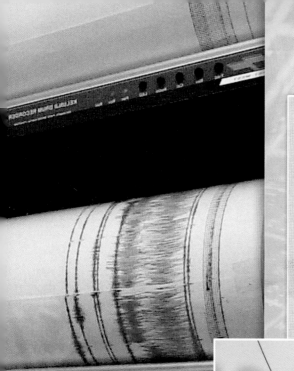

This volcanologist is keeping an eye on a seismograph. It measures the shaking of the ground around the volcano.

Map Key

- Active volcano   Ring of Fire

Q CHALLENGE QUESTIONS

One of the other volcanologists tells you that she has visited several other volcanoes so far this year. She circles their locations on a map.

1. How many volcanoes did she visit in the Ring of Fire?

2. Two of the volcanoes she visited are not in the Ring of Fire. On which plates are they located?

3. On which plate is most of the United States located?

4. Look at the cross-section of Earth on page 14. Which layer is thicker: the mantle or the inner core?

5. Look at the cross-section of Earth on page 14. What is the layer at the center of Earth called?

A volcano's shape can change when it is close to erupting. You use instruments to monitor changes in the volcano. A few days ago, you placed an electronic distance meter (EDM) on the volcano. Now it's time to check the data the EDM has been collecting. A helicopter takes you to the base of the volcano, where the EDM is located. You gather the information you need. Your next stop is halfway up the volcano. You want to set up another instrument, called a tiltmeter.

You can see a bulge on the left of this volcano.

FACTFILE

Magma inside a volcano is under great pressure. As magma rises, it puts pressure on the rock around it. That can cause the surface of the volcano to change in appearance. Deformation is a change in the height of the land around the volcano.

A. The changes may be large, such as a bulge in the volcano's side.

B. Sometimes an area on the sides may sink in.

C. Some changes are small, such as a slight difference in the tilt, or slope, of the land.

WORKSTATION

You check on the electronic distance meter (EDM). This instrument records changes in the surface of the volcano.

A volcanologist takes an EDM reading.

- EDMs are set up around the volcano to monitor changes on each side.
- The EDM aims a laser beam at a reflector on the side of the volcano. The beam is reflected back to the EDM. The EDM then calculates the angle of the slope.
- You compare data from the last several days. It shows that the angle of the ground has changed. That means the pressure from the rising magma has changed the shape of the volcano.

A scientist installs a tiltmeter on a volcano.

On the side of the volcano, you dig a hole for the tiltmeter.

- Tiltmeters record changes in the angle, or tilt, of the ground.
- Tiltmeters are planted in shallow holes in the ground. This holds them in place when the ground moves as a bulge forms.
- The data the tiltmeters collect is sent out as radio waves. The data is picked up by a passing satellite and sent to scientists at the observatory.

Q CHALLENGE QUESTIONS

During the last week, data from an EDM has shown a growing bulge in the side of the volcano.

1. What is causing the bulge?
2. Why are EDMs set up in several different locations?
3. What data would you expect to gather from a tiltmeter located near the bulge?
4. Why is the tiltmeter partly buried and not just sitting on the ground?
5. How does the data get from the tiltmeter to the laboratory?

The helicopter has dropped you off near the crater. Gas and steam are rising out of the ground. You don't want to breathe in these gases. They are very bad for your health. Besides, the area smells like rotten eggs! The conditions for gathering gas samples are perfect today. The volcano seems calm and the weather is good. You have a helicopter waiting to take you to safety in case the volcano's activity increases.

FACTFILE

As you gather samples, volcanic gases are all around you. Water vapor, carbon dioxide, and sulfur dioxide are the most common.

- Volcanic gases are dissolved in the underground magma.
- They form bubbles and escape as the magma rises to the surface.
- They seep out through openings called fumaroles. They also escape through the ground and vents.
- Some volcanic gases are poisonous. They can even harm plants and animals that are several miles away.
- Gases may be released long before an eruption begins. Sometimes they continue for hundreds or thousands of years after it ends.

The gases and heat can kill trees.

Fumaroles are openings in the ground through which gases and steam escape.

A gas mask will protect you from breathing in dangerous gases.

WORKSTATION

As you collect gas samples, you are looking for changes in certain gases.

- As magma rises to the surface, different gases are released. That tells you that an eruption could happen soon.

There are several ways to measure the contents of volcanic gas.

- Samples can be taken as gas escapes from the ground.

- Specially equipped airplanes and satellites can measure the gases that rise from the volcano.

- Measurements can be taken by instruments set up near an area where gases are escaping. The instruments are left to run on their own.

- Samples of soil can show the levels of gases in the soil.

Q CHALLENGE QUESTIONS

1. What are the three most common volcanic gases?
2. Volcanic gases can continue to be released for how long after an eruption?
3. What are fumaroles?
4. What are you looking for when you collect samples of volcanic gases?
5. Why should you wear a gas mask when collecting volcanic gases?

SHAKY GROUND

You have a few more stops to make before getting off the volcano. You want to check on the seismometers you set up at different locations. A seismometer is an instrument that detects and records the shaking of the ground during an earthquake. Earthquakes usually happen before and during an eruption. Later, you will look at a printout of the information collected by the seismometer. It shows the kind of earthquakes that have happened. Some quakes can give clues that a volcano is about to erupt!

Scientists use seismometers on volcanoes all over the world and in all weather.

FACTFILE

While you are on the mountain, you check on one other piece of equipment: the crackmeter.

- Sometimes the movement of the ground causes cracks to form.
- The crackmeter measures if the cracks are getting wider or narrower.
- The instrument consists of a bar that is placed across the crack. It is held in place by anchors at each end.
- The width of the crack is measured by a gauge.

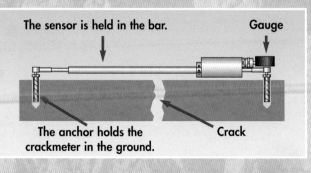

The sensor is held in the bar.   Gauge

The anchor holds the crackmeter in the ground.   Crack

WORKSTATION

The ground shakes a bit beneath your feet. Could it be magma moving underground?

- As magma moves underground, it pushes aside solid rock and causes the ground to shake. Shallow earthquakes usually take place both before and during the eruption of a volcano.
- The seismometer measures the shaking as electronic signals.
- The signals are sent to the laboratory. There, the recorded information is printed out. The printout is called a seismogram.
- The data can tell you the time, location, depth, and magnitude (strength) of the earthquake.
- The data from a seismometer can be used to track the movement of magma underground.

You're looking at seismograms from the last few weeks. The zigzag lines on the printouts tell you there have been four different types of earthquakes.

Earthquakes deep in Earth's crust show up as jagged lines that start close together and spread out.

This shows shallow earthquakes at the center of the volcano's crater. The vibrations are large and spread out.

Surface movements, such as rockfalls and landslides, start small and get larger. You can see that same pattern in the lines.

This shows long-lasting steady shaking called harmonic tremors. They often occur around active volcanoes.

Q CHALLENGE QUESTIONS

1. What kind of quakes or ground movements do these seismograms show?

A.

B.

C.

D.

2. What does the crackmeter measure?

21

ERUPTION ALERT

Ever since the volcano started showing signs of erupting, the people living nearby have been on alert. Local officials have been urging people to leave. No one knows for sure what will happen to the villages on the island when the volcano erupts. Steam and gases are rising from the crater. The earthquakes are getting stronger. Even so, some people still don't want to leave their homes. You put out another warning. Everyone must get out now!

Every available vehicle is used to get people out of the villages.

FACTFILE

Many local residents decided to leave because of your warnings.

- A refugee center is set up. People who leave their homes can stay there and be safe.
- Officials are searching every house to make sure that nobody has stayed behind.
- All roads near the volcano are closed.
- An emergency search-and-rescue crew is on alert.

Rescue workers help evacuate residents.

WORKSTATION

You are very concerned that the coming eruption will trigger a deadly mudflow called a lahar.

This picture shows a mudflow caused by a volcano erupting in Colombia, in 1985. This mudflow completely destroyed a village.

- A lahar is a thick mudflow. It is made of water mixed with volcanic ash, rock, and mud.
- A mudflow looks like wet cement pouring down the slopes of a volcano.
- It can carry rocks of all sizes, from tiny pieces of clay to boulders that are 30 feet (9 m) across.
- A lahar can be hundreds of feet wide. It can flow as fast as 40 miles (64 km) per hour. Some mudflows travel as far as 50 miles (80 km).
- A lahar picks up more water and rock as it flows. It can grow to 10 times its original size.

A mudflow at the Galunggung volcano, in Indonesia, in 1982

Various factors could cause a lahar.

- It could be caused by the sudden melting of snow and ice during an eruption.
- Shaking ground might loosen a section of the mountain. If the earth breaks free in a landslide, it could slide into a river or lake. Water spilling over the banks of a river or lake could then start a lahar.
- Sometimes the shaking ground causes a lake to break over its banks and spill.
- A heavy rain can start a lahar. It can wash away rock that was deposited or shaken loose during an eruption.

Q CHALLENGE QUESTIONS

1. Why is a house-to-house search necessary?
2. What is a lahar?
3. How could a lahar grow to 10 times its original size?
4. How fast can a lahar travel? How far?
5. How can a lahar be caused by the heat of a volcano?

23

EYEWITNESS TO AN ERUPTION

The volcano erupts with a huge blast. One side of the mountain collapses. You watch in awe from the safety of the observatory. You are also very busy studying the data as it comes in. You measure and record data and take pictures as this amazing event unfolds around you. You hear that a lake has burst over its banks. The flood of water has mixed with hot ash. A lahar is now gushing downhill toward the village!

FACTFILE

Volcanic eruptions can bury entire towns in several ways.

- During and after an eruption, ash can fill the air. People may have trouble breathing. Some cities have been buried in ash up to 10 feet (3 m) deep.

- A lahar can drown a town in a mix of water, mud, ash and rocks.

A deadly lahar buried this town. Rescue workers survey the damage.

Types of Tephra

This volcano is blasting out a huge amount of tephra. Tephra can take many forms, from tiny ashes to large blocks.

- **Ash** is the smallest kind of tephra. It ranges from very fine to rather coarse grains. Ash rises in a cloud above the volcano. It also blows away, filling the air for miles around.

- **Lapilli** are pebble-like fragments of tephra. They are larger than a pea but smaller than a walnut.

- **Blocks** are larger chunks of rock with sharp sides. They can measure more than a foot in width. Blocks were solid when they were blown out of the volcano.

- **Bombs** began as molten lava shot from the volcano. The lava fragments cooled and hardened as they flew through the air. They developed a rounded, pear shape.

- **Pumice** is a volcanic rock. It is formed from lava. Lava is full of gas. When the lava cools, the gas escapes and leaves behind tiny holes. The holes make pumice very light in weight.

Q CHALLENGE QUESTIONS

Look at "Types of Tephra" above and answer the following questions.

1. Which type of tephra is so small and light that it can be blown away?
2. The volcano spits out jagged chunks of rock more than a foot wide. What type of tephra are they?
3. You find a chunk of volcanic rock. It is very light and has holes on its surface. What is it called?
4. You pick up a fragment that is about the size of a marble. What type of tephra is it?
5. How are tephra bombs formed?

When the eruption began, a column of hot ash burst with great force from the vent. In less than 10 minutes, it had risen more than 10 miles (16 km) into the air. It also carried chunks of rock and cooling lava skyward, spitting them out in all directions. Now it is topped by a growing ash cloud, also known as an eruption cloud or plume. You watch to see which direction the wind will carry the cloud.

This ash cloud is a dark brownish-gray. Ash clouds can also be white or light gray.

FACTFILE

- During an eruption, steam and other expanding gases force material out of the vent.
- The ash column usually rises straight up and then spreads sideways to form a cloud.
- Depending on the size of the eruption, an ash cloud may last minutes or months.

Ash clouds carry less tephra as time goes on.

Pyroclastic Flow

Pyroclastic flow is a thick cloud of volcanic gases, ash, and rock that rolls down the mountain like an avalanche. It can be one of the deadliest parts of an eruption. However, not all eruptions cause a pyroclastic flow.

- A pyroclastic flow forms when a cloud of hot volcanic gases, ash, and pieces of volcanic rock becomes so heavy that it collapses. The flow rolls down the volcano at a speed of 60 miles (100 km) per hour or more.

- The temperature inside the flow may reach 1,200° F (649° C). The flow quickly covers many square miles.

- Ash and volcanic rock form layers up to 60 feet (18 m) deep.

- The flow can strip trees from hillsides as far as 6 miles (10 km) from the crater. Trees may be knocked down and snapped in half for miles around. Farther away, trees are left standing but are killed by the intense heat.

The pyroclastic flow rolls along the ground and in the air.

You study the measurements you have taken of the ash cloud since the eruption started.

Time	9 A.M.	10 A.M.	11 A.M.	12 P.M.	1 P.M.	2 P.M.	3 P.M.	4 P.M.
Height (ft)	0	5,000	7,500	9,000	10,000	12,500	14,500	15,000

CHALLENGE QUESTIONS

1. What causes a pyroclastic flow to form?

2. How high can the temperature inside a pyroclastic flow reach?

3. Look at the chart above. During which time period did the ash cloud rise the fastest?

4. How long did it take the cloud to reach 15,000 feet?

ERUPTION AFTERMATH

As soon as it is safe to do so, you return to the village. It has been completely destroyed. You've seen the aftermath of an eruption many times. Still, you never get used to the destruction. There is some good news, though. The refugee center reports that everyone from the village is safe. You think of other volcanic eruptions, when thousands of people were killed or injured. You are glad that you could warn these villagers in time.

> After the eruption, a thick layer of fine gray ash fills the air and covers everything in sight.

FACTFILE

Here's a look at devastating eruptions of the past.

- In A.D. 79, Mount Vesuvius erupted in Italy. Pyroclastic flow buried the ancient Roman town of Pompeii and everyone who lived there.

- In 1883, the volcanic island Krakatau erupted in Indonesia. It was one of the most violent eruptions in history. Two-thirds of the island of Krakatau collapsed. The effects of a huge ash cloud were felt around the world. About 36,000 people died.

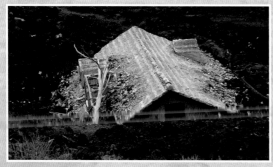

Sometimes it's too dangerous to rebuild after an eruption.

People are your first priority.

- Villagers need food, clothing, and shelter. Help will soon pour in from all over the world.
- Some villagers have developed health problems because of the ash in the air. Some have difficulty breathing. Other people have eye infections. A clinic will be set up to help these people.
- It may not be possible for anyone to return to the village. The volcano could be active for years. You suggest rebuilding in another location, far away from the danger of the volcano.

At first, plants will not be able to grow in volcanic ash. But over time, the ash breaks down to become rich soil that is ideal for plants.

- The volcanic ash is made up of minerals that plants cannot use. In time, however, these minerals break apart and release nutrients into the soil.
- The nutrients are all important for the growth of plants. They make the soil very fertile.

This shoot is growing in volcanic ash.

Q CHALLENGE QUESTIONS

1. What happened to the island of Krakatau after an eruption in 1883?
2. What kind of health problems can be caused by ash?
3. Why can't plants grow in the volcanic ash at first?
4. People often grow crops on the slopes of volcanoes. Why do you think that is?

Pages 6–7
Volcanologist on Duty

A volcano is either active or extinct. If it has erupted in the last 10,000 years, it's active. If it hasn't, it's extinct. An active volcano may not have erupted for a long time, even hundreds of years. Such a volcano is said to be active but dormant, or "sleeping." It could erupt again!

Pages 8–9
Varieties of Volcanoes

Both stratovolcanoes and cinder cones are cone-shaped. Both have steep sides. What's the difference between them? One big difference is the way their sides are built up. Check out the FACTFILE for that information.

You may have heard of a composite volcano. That's just another name for a stratovolcano.

Pages 12–13
Volcanic Island

You'll find several different pieces of information in the WORKSTATION chart. It gives the name of the volcano, its location, and even an actual photograph. Be sure to pay attention to the eruption year. A couple of volcanoes are listed more than once. It's the same mountain, but different eruptions took place at different times!

Pages 14–15
Ring of Fire

There is a very close connection between volcanoes and earthquakes. Both are often the result of movement of tectonic plates. About 90 percent of the world's earthquakes take place along the Ring of Fire.

Pages 18–19
Right at the Rim

When a volcano is close to erupting, the amount of gases escaping may increase. Volcanologists are looking for something else when they collect gas samples. They want to find out what different types of gases are being given off. How are they mixed ? How concentrated are they? These things may change as the volcano gets closer to erupting.

Pages 20–21
Shaky Ground

No two seismograms from different earthquakes look exactly alike. A volcanologist reading a seismogram studies the patterns. Seismograms from the same type of earthquake will show some of the same patterns. There will also be some differences.

Pages 22–23
Eruption Alert

There's a good reason that a lahar looks like wet concrete as it flows. Concrete is made of finely ground mineral material, plus water, sand, and gravel or crushed stone. That's very similar to the materials found in a lahar.

Pages 24–25
Eyewitness to an Eruption

Types of tephra are grouped according to size. Though their size may be similar, types within a group can look very different. They can be made of different materials or cooled in different ways.

Pages 26–27
Ash Clouds

An ash column will rise until it reaches a level where it is the same density as the surrounding air. Then it spreads out sideways to form a cloud. Leftover energy may cause it to rise a little higher.

ANSWERS

Pages 6–7
1. Lava; magma
2. Through the chimney
3. Gases, ash, and hardened lava
4. No, because an extinct volcano is not likely ever to erupt again

Pages 8–9
1. Hardened bits of lava build up around the vent.
2. They are formed from layers of lava, ash, and volcanic rocks.
3. Pelean
4. Hawaiian

Pages 10–11
1. 2,200° F (1,200° C)
2. Pillow lava
3. Aa lava
4. Pillow lava
5. Pahoehoe lava

Pages 12–13
1. 3–15 km; every 100+ years
2. Mount Pinatubo; VEI-6
3. Reventador in 2002 and 2004

Pages 14–15
1. Three
2. On the African Plate and Eurasian Plate
3. North American Plate
4. The mantle
5. The inner core

Pages 16–17
1. Magma rising inside the volcano pushes against the rock and causes it to bulge outward.
2. To monitor changes on each side of the volcano
3. A difference in the angle (tilt) of the land
4. To keep it in place as the ground around it moves
5. It sends radio waves to a satellite, which sends the data on to the observatory.

Pages 18–19
1. Water vapor, carbon dioxide, and sulfur dioxide
2. Thousands of years
3. Openings in the ground through which volcanic gases and steam escape
4. Changes in certain gases that may show that an eruption could happen soon
5. Some of the gases are dangerous to breathe.

Pages 20–21
1. A. Shallow earthquake at the center of a volcano
   B. Harmonic tremor
   C. Deep earthquake under Earth's crust
   D. Surface movement, such as a landslide or rockfall
2. The crackmeter measures the width of cracks caused by the movement of the ground.

Pages 22–23
1. To be sure that no one has stayed behind
2. A lahar is a thick mudflow of water, volcanic ash, rock, and mud.
3. The lahar can pick up more water and rock as it flows.
4. 40 miles (64 km) per hour; up to 50 miles (80 km)
5. The heat causes snow and ice on the volcano to melt quickly.

Pages 24–25
1. Ash
2. Blocks
3. Pumice
4. Lapilli
5. They begin as molten lava and cool off as they fly through the air.

Pages 26–27
1. The ash cloud becomes heavy and collapses.
2. 1,200° F (649° C)
3. 9 A.M. to 10 A.M.
4. Seven hours

Pages 28–29
1. Two-thirds of the island collapsed.
2. Ash may cause breathing problems and eye infections.
3. At first, the volcanic ash is made up of minerals that plants cannot use.
4. Volcanic soil eventually becomes very rich and ideal for plants.

ASH CLOUD gases, ash, and rock fragments that rise into the air during a volcanic eruption; also known as an eruption cloud or plume

CRATER a steep-sided, usually bowl-shaped depression at the summit of a volcano

DEFORMATION a change in the shape of a material, caused by pressure, strain, or stress

EVACUATE to leave an area to avoid danger

FAULT a crack in Earth's crust where huge blocks of rock slide past each other

FUMAROLE a volcanic vent through which volcanic gases escape

LAHAR a type of mudflow that begins on the side of a volcano when water, volcanic ash, and rocks combine and flow rapidly downhill

LAVA molten matter from a volcano or a break in Earth's surface. Before it reaches the surface, it is known as magma.

MAGMA molten rock in Earth's mantle and outer core. Magma that reaches the surface is called lava.

MAGNITUDE a measurement of the energy released during an earthquake

MANTLE the thick layer of Earth that lies beneath the crust

MINERAL a solid inorganic (nonliving) material substance that occurs naturally on Earth

NUTRIENT a substance that plants and animals need to grow and develop

OBSERVATORY a building designed for observing something

PRESSURE a physical force put on or against an object, from something touching it

PYROCLASTIC FLOW an extremely hot mixture of ash, gas, and volcanic rock fragments that travels at high speed down the sides of a volcano or along the surface of the ground

SEISMOGRAM the printed record of information recorded by a seismograph

SEISMOGRAPH an instrument that detects, measures, and records the vibrations caused by an earthquake

SEISMOMETER an instrument that measures the vibrations of Earth at a specific location

TECTONIC PLATES giant pieces of Earth's crust that float on Earth's mantle. They are always moving at a very slow rate.

TEPHRA rock material of all sizes that is thrown into the air during an eruption

VENT an opening at Earth's surface through which volcanic materials erupt

VOLCANIC FIELD an area of Earth's crust that contains several volcanoes

PICTURE CREDITS
(l = left, r = right, t = top, c = center, b = bottom)

Cover: Shutterstock. **Alamy:** 16–17 (main), 22–23 (main). **Corbis:** title page, 6–7 (main) Bettmann/Corbis, 10–11, 10b, 13tl, 18–19 (main), 22b Reuters/Corbis, 24–25 (main), 24b, 25ct, 25cb, 28b Reuters/Corbis, 30–31 (main), 30l, 32 (main). **Getty:** 13cl, 13c, 14–15 (main) Dinodia Picture Agency, 29t AFP/Getty, 28–29 (main) AFP/Getty. **iStockPhoto:** 25t. **NOAA:** 13bl. **Oregon State University:** 19b. **Photoatlas:** 13bc. **Rex Features:** 23tr. **Science Photo Library:** 8–9 (main), 19t, 20–21 (main), 23cl W.K. Fletcher/Science Photo Library, 27t. **Shutterstock:** cover, 6c iofoto, 11t, 11b, 12–13 (main), 16b Lisa F. Young, 19rt, 26–27 (main). **Still Pictures:** 29cl H. Buesemann/Still Pictures. **USGS:** 8t, 8c, 8b, 13tr, 17t, 17c, 18c, 18b, 19cb, 26b. **ticktock media archive:** 7c, 9ft, 9t, 9c, 9b, 9fb, 14b, 15c, 16b, 20b. **Wikimedia:** 11c, 13tc, 13cr, 13br, 25b.

Every effort has been made to trace the copyright holders, and we apologize in advance for any unintentional omissions. We would be pleased to insert the appropriate acknowledgments in any subsequent edition of this publication.